rhode island

eat

D1086711

cafe zelda

best little cafe between bar harbor and key west

528 thames street. corner of dean
401.849.4002 www.cafezelda.com
mon - thu 3 - 10p sat - sun 11a - 10p

opened in 1986. owners: tom and roxanne callahan chef: john philcox
$$: mc. visa
lunch. dinner. brunch. full bar. reservations recommended

newport > **e1**

so murph walks into a bar, and steve the bartender says, "hey, murph, what'll it be, the usual?" this is not the setup for a joke. this is just another weekday afternoon at *cafe zelda*. i assume you'll be going to the restaurant, as i did, for the chicken-fried lobster. smart move. i'm certain you'll enjoy it. but don't pass up the bar on your way out. it's got the real honest bar vibe that takes years, sometimes decades, to flourish.

imbibe:
dark & stormy with milligan's island
  newport ginger beer
the diesel: espresso, cuervo & tia maria

devour:
cafe zelda burger
nori-wrapped ahi tuna
chicken-fried lobster
superlative sakonnet river oysters with sake

chez pascal

innovative modern french

960 hope street. corner of ninth
401.421.4422 www.chez-pascal.com
tue - sat 5:30 - 9:30p

opened in 2003. owners: matthew & kristin gennuso chef: matthew gennuso
$$$: all major credit cards accepted
dinner. full bar. reservations recommended

providence : hope street > **e2**

true or not, we've come to believe that the french dine out with their children more often and more unapologetically than we americans. this is why, when our first daughter gwen was just weeks old, we went to *chez pascal* for our first outing. nestled in her bjorn, with a napkin draped over her head, gwen was welcomed by both owners and patrons alike. naturally, the food was flawless. to many, *chez pascal* is an anniversary, serious date or celebration restaurant. to us, it's just our neighborhood family joint.

imbibe:
hendrick's gin with cucumber sorbet
16 wines by the glass

devour:
pork belly with potato & sauerkraut torte
bomster sea scallops
crispy duck leg confit with wilted
  red cabbage, watercress & sour cherries
pear upside-down cake with blue cheese

costantino's ristorante

al fresco dining in the heart of providence's italian section

265 atwells avenue. corner of depasquale square
401.528.1100 www.vendaravioli.com
mon - thu 5 - 10p fri - sat 5 - 11p sun 5 - 9p

opened in 2002. owners: alan costantino executive chef: alberto lopez
$$ - $$$: all major credit cards accepted
dinner. full bar. reservations recommended

providence : federal hill > **e3**

have you looked at the price of an airline ticket lately? insanity. the truly savvy traveler will take my advice and head instead to federal hill, about 30 minutes before the sun sets. once there, grab a seat at *costantino's*, order a prosecco bellini, eat to excess the various primi and secondi, and, to complete the italian fantasy, spend the night at a nearby b&b on depasquale square. so you won't have actually gone to italy, but you'll be happier because you've had a beautiful meal and you'll be a few thousand bucks richer.

imbibe:
bellini with prosecco
moretti beer

devour:
insalata costantino d'estate
antipasto della casa
insalata di scungilli
pollo alla sienese
ravioli con aragosta

eastside marketplace

a local grocer that gets it right

165 pitman street. corner of gano
401.831.7771 www.eastsidemarket.com
mon - sun 8a - 10p

opened in 1981. owner: scott laurans
$$: all major credit cards accepted
grocery

providence : east side >

since this is a guide to stylish eating and shopping, why not go a grocery store where you can do either or both? *eastside marketplace* truly gets the "think local" premise. while many other grocers are consolidating, *eastside* continues to be family-owned and run. they are committed to the community and offer a range of helpful services including parcel pickup and delivery. recently, they've begun offering organic and conventional produce at the same prices. now, that shows style!

imbibe:
autocrat coffee syrup
rhody fresh whole milk

devour:
local asparagus
free bakery cookies for the kids
storemade italian sausage
raspberry rugelach
rotisserie chicken

farmstead

outstanding cheese and cheese accessories

186 wayland avenue. corner of waterman
401.274.7177 www.farmsteadinc.com
tue - sat 10a - 7p

opened in 2003. owner: matt and kate jennings
$$ - $$$: all major credit cards accepted
grocery

providence : wayland square > **e5**

"to brie or not to brie" is not a question worth puzzling over. the answer is always yes, and doubly so, when it's a double cream brie, as you might find at *farmstead*. and triply so, when... well, you know. many other questions can be answered at *farmstead* too. crucial questions like, "where do i find a gril raclette for an an apres ski party?" and, "is there anybody who makes really quality cheeseboards in rhode island?" these questions and many more, including the deepest existential question, "is cheese really what life is all about?" can be answered here.

devour:
montgomery's extra mature cow cheddar
blue ledge farm goat's milk crottina
nesting butters, jams & preserves
matiz paella rice
caffe-tassé chocolate bars
farmstead signature spices

garden grille

all vegetarian and vegan, all the time
727 east avenue. corner of pidge avenue
401.726.2826 www.gardengrillecafe.com
mon - thur 11a - 9:30p fri - sat 11a - 10p sun 10a - 9:30p

opened in 1996. owner: robert yaffe chef: jonathan dille
$$: all major credit cards accepted
lunch. dinner. brunch. first come, first served

pawtucket > **e6**

once in a while i like to do a healthy thing. when the urge strikes, i want to make sure that that healthy thing is memorable. eating at *garden grille* satisfies this need. the daily menu items are consistently interesting and good, but the specials are especially creative. as a pretty committed carnivore, i doubt i'll ever switch over to "the other side," but it's nice to know that there are great alternatives out there if i do.

imbibe:
kauai kiss smoothie
organic carrot, beet & parsley juice

devour:
buddha bowl with tofu in a miso ginger sauce
sea vegetable salad
squash quesadilla
pizza bella with mushrooms & artichokes
vegan chocolate mousse pie

garrison confections

handmade chocolates and chocolate-inspired gifts

815 hope street. corner of fourth
401.490.2740 www.garrisonconfections.com
mon - fri 11a - 6:30p   sat 11a - 5p

opened in 2004. owner/chef: andrew shotts
$$ - $$$: all major credit cards accepted
treats

providence : hope street > **e7**

let's start with the décor at *garrison confections*. brownest brown and orangest orange. it's always fall in my world, so the color palette alone beckoned me in. then the chocolate. serious, thoughtful, hard-core chocolate. personally, i don't need to study chocolate like these guys do. i'll trust them if they tell me it's some kind of single-estate, exotic rare bean. whatever. more, please.

imbibe:
ultimate spicy hot chocolate
milk laced with guittard caramel syrup

devour:
rocky rhode island
coffee milk tablet
chocolate caramel corn
guittard chocolate chips
ultimate nougat bar

hotel manisses

a lovely restaurant indoors and out

1 spring street. corner of high
401.466.2421 www.blockislandresorts.com
mon - sun 5:30 - 9:30p

opened in 1976. owners: the abrams and draper families chef: ross audino
$$ - $$$: all major credit cards accepted
dinner. full bar. reservations recommended

block island > **e8**

when i'm on island, i like to trust the locals. (i also like to say things like "on island" because it makes me feel kinda silly but at the same time secretly cool). when the locals told me that *hotel manisses* is where it's at, as several did, i was inclined to believe them. they were right. i had a sublime meal there, outdoors on that impossibly beautiful island, surrounded by ridiculously lovely views. perhaps next time, i won't go off island at all, but extend my visit at the hotel.

imbibe:
sangria martini
v.s. sidecar

devour:
truffle roasted bay scallops with artichoke
lobster salad with tarragon aioli
foie gras & poached pear
brie & crab stuffed beef tenderloin
chocolate fondue with fruit & cake

17

hudson street market

mom and pop corner store and deli

68 hudson street. corner of sycamore
401.274.4540 www.kitiyakara.com/world/hudson.htm
mon - fri 7a - 7p sat 8a - 7p sun 8a - 4p

opened in 1922. owners: khym and john carmichael
$: mc. visa
lunch. dinner. grocery. first come, first served

providence : west side > **e9**

if you're of a certain age (as i was, some years ago), then you appreciate the "norm concept." you walk into a place, and everybody knows your name. i love that. at *hudson street market*, eric and khym know everybody. they know their customers' sandwich preferences, vacation plans and dating habits. plus, they make a mean vegetarian sandwich, a concept i didn't even acknowledge before i began eating theirs. keep on keeping on with those olives, khym.

imbibe:
aj olde style raspberry lime rickey
hudson street house blend mocha java
  "not chocolate flavored"

devour:
vegetarian sandwich on pumpernickel
buffalo chicken breast on bakery white
italian grinder
copocolla sandwich on sourdough

julian's

funky artsy adventuresome comfort food

318 broadway. corner of vinton
401.861.1770 www.superfineproductions.com
mon - fri 9a - 11p sat - sun brunch 9am - 3pm dinner 5 - 11pm

opened in 1996. owner: julian forge
$$: all major credit cards accepted
brunch. lunch. dinner. first come, first served

providence : west side > **e10**

it's morning. you're hungover. what do you want to eat? *julian's* hash. it's lunch. you ran today, and you're feeling healthy. what do you want to eat? *julian's* tempeh wrap. it's evening. you've got friends visiting from somewhere really cool. what do you want to eat? *julian's* board special. it's sunday brunch. your snobby, impossible-to-please father-in-law is in town. what do you want to eat? a *julian's* bloody mary for you and *julian's* salmon benedict for him. *julian's*. forever.

imbibe:
mango cosmo
strawberry mimosa

devour:
sirloin with tempura-battered cauliflower
scallion almond pancakes stuffed with
  apples, tempeh sausage & rice noodles
italian french toast
lemon & blackberry tart

la creperie

paris meets providence on a side street
82 fones alley. corner of thayer
401.751.5536
mon - thu, sun 10a - midnight fri - sat 10a - 2a

opened in 1996. chef/owner: leslie carnevale
$$: all major credit cards accepted
breakfast. lunch. dinner. late night. first come, first served

providence > **e11**

oh, sure, my husband and i own a fancy-pants belgian waffle maker. useless. who has the foresight to prepare the yeasted batter the night before? and homemade crepes? more like biodegradable confetti in my hands. that's why *la creperie* is indispensable when you need that yeasty, toothsome platform for oozing toppings. and, of course, i don't limit myself to breakfast. not when i know leslie is over there working her brie-and-apple crepe magic all day long.

imbibe:
cranberry cooler
tropical oasis smoothie

devour:
crepe with apple & brie
belgian waffle with apple cinnamon & sugar
the catherine crepe with chicken & onions
the chiara crepe with nutella
the betty crepe with butter & sugar

23

la laiterie

wine, beer and cheese bar featuring seasonal, handcrafted food

188 wayland avenue. corner of waterman
401.274.7177 www.lalaiterie.farmsteadinc.com
restaurant tue - sat 5 - 11p store tue - sat 10a - 7p

opened in 2006. owners: matt and kate jennings chef: matt jennings
$$ - $$$: all major credit cards accepted
dinner. first come, first served

providence : wayland square > e12

stinky cheese and beer. and bread. stinky cheese, beer and bread. when i cross over to the "other side," that's what i want put inside my sarcophagus, à la the egyptians, who, by the way, did include beer and bread in their tombs. i'd add some wine. and maybe a really outstanding burger. with a side of polenta frites. better still, simply entomb me in *la laiterie*, and i will undoubtedly make a happy passage and be content for all eternity.

imbibe:
curds 'n' whey double ipa
saison au point

devour:
sticky washed & stinky cheese plate
1/2 pound vermont burger
cheesemonger's mac & cheese with
   a crusty top
organic strawberry johnnycake cobbler

lili marlene's

noir-ish bar with pool and po' boys

422 atwells avenue. corner of marcello
401.751.4996
sun - thu 4p - 1a fri - sat 4p - 2a

opened in 2002. owner: michael saers
$ - $$: all major credit cards accepted
dinner. late night. full bar. first come, first served

providence : federal hill > e13

for the full-on dark bar drinking and socializing experience, *lilli marlene's* can't be beat. rich velvet curtains block out all of the sunlight, and dimmed lights keep sight to a minimum. it's true what they say; in the absence of seeing, your other senses take over. food smells better. drinks taste better. maybe that's why i like *lili's* so much. it appeals to all my senses.

imbibe:
perfect sidecar
genesee cream ale on tap

devour:
shrimp po' boy
bacon cheeseburger with fries
peel & eat shrimp
tomato caprese salad
chicken breast sandwich

lucky garden

good chinese, both exotic and domestic

1852 smith street. corner of allen
401.231.5626 www.luckyandpearl.com
mon - thu 11:30a - 10p fri - sat 11a - 11p sun 11a - 10p

opened in 1991. owner: sherri ho
$ - $$: all major credit cards accepted
lunch. dinner. first come, first served

north providence > **e14**

part of the appeal of *lucky garden* is the secret hand-shake bit. i'm a sucker for that "in the know" thing. before, i might have come in and ordered *lucky garden's* very finest chop suey, and it would have been better than most chop suey around rhode island. but now, in possession of the code, i can come in and say, "hong kong menu, please." and then, like the sudden shift to color in the wizard of oz, the world becomes a brighter place. tastier too, thanks to dishes like the taro preserved duck.

imbibe:
housemade sweet soybean milk
shirley temple

devour:
seafood in crispy taro bowl
steamed pork shanghai dumplings
crispy roast chicken
house special pork with preserved mustard
pepper salt fried squids

milk & honey bazaar

artisan cheeses and charcuterie in a rural setting

3838 main road / route 77
401.624.1974 www.milkandhoneybazaar.com
mon - fri 10a - 6p sat 10a - 5p sun noon - 5p (closed mon - tue sept to june)

opened in 2004. owners: tom and jennifer jansen
$$: all major credit cards accepted
lunch. grocery. first come, first served

tiverton > **e15**

i worked for country living magazine for a while in the '90s and now get rashes when i see too much country rustic stuff. *milk and honey* manages to provide all that's right with country living: fresh eggs, local cheese and artisan honey. and they blend in all that's right elsewhere, too, like sophisticated olive oils, crackers, and pâtés. *milk and honey* is all wholesome yumminess without a faux-distressed, milk-painted cupboard in sight.

imbibe:
organic limeaid from spain
lorina sparkling orangeade

devour:
martin's family goat cheese
great hill blue cow cheese
piave vecchio cow cheese
cashel blue cow cheese
petit basque sheep cheese

mill's tavern

top-notch food and service
99 - 101 n main street. corner of angell
401.272.3331
mon - thu 5 - 10p fri - sat 5 - 11p sun 4 - 9p

opened in 2003. owner: jamie d'oliveira chef: corey french
$$$: all major credit cards accepted
dinner. full bar. reservations recommended

providence : college hill > **e16**

that short rib you're looking at. that one there on the left—almost didn't sit still for this photo session. it was cooked so brilliantly that each time i adjusted the plate for the shot, that tender, tender meat would quake ever so gently, and i would have to pause and wait for it to settle. it almost proved true the cliché "falling off the bone." it is also true to say that i fall all over myself for the opportunity to eat at *mill's tavern*.

imbibe:
pear & pomegranate caipiranha
tire iron with maker's mark & bitters

devour:
pan roasted mushrooms with madeira & thyme
crispy salmon
braised short rib
pommery mustard & horseradish rack of lamb
vanilla ricotta cheesecake

33

modern diner

classic retro diner with modern flair

364 east avenue. corner of patt street
401.726.8390
mon - sat 6a - 2p sun 7a - 2p

opened in 1985. owners: nick and frank
$$: cash
breakfast. lunch. first come, first served

pawtucket > **e17**

on my first visit to rhode island, i ate at this venerable breakfast place. that was eight years ago, and then, as now, i stood in a long line and tried to memorize the thumbtacked specials before being seated at a booth in the main car. back then, i marveled that each elaborate breakfast was served with a cheery orchid or a fresh sprig of rosemary on top of layers of custards, sauces and syrups. now, i just eat and enjoy, and i, in turn, bring my friends to *modern diner* when they visit.

imbibe:
orange juice mimosa
cup o' joe

devour:
belgian waffle with fruit
mexican eggs
pesto cheese grits
italian sausage with eggs
french toast with custard

mumu cuisine

stylish chinese dining on the hill

220 atwells avenue. corner of dean
401.369.7041
mon, wed, thu, sun 11:30a - 10:30p fri - sat 11:30a - 11:30p

opened in 2006. owners: henry mu and sophia cuyegkeng   chef: lao sun
$$: all major credit cards accepted
lunch. dinner. full bar. reservations recommended

providence : federal hill > e18

i understand that there are exceptions to this, but if i really like the décor at a place then i'm more inclined to like the food. take *mumu cuisine*, where the color of the walls alone inspires my appetite. sophia's walls are the richest most luxe red-orange. they're neither red nor orange but a combustible fusion. when someone uses a color that bold, i trust that they'll use the same daring on the menu. and with the help of the chef, lured from one of the tonier restaurants in beijing, *mumu's* does not disappoint. suddenly atwells avenue is home to some of the best chinese in the region.

imbibe:
flyin' hawaiian
warm tea

devour:
green tea fried rice with bacon
tofu piano
prawns in silky cream with walnuts
xiao longbao
crispy beef

nat porter

modern food in an 18th century building
125 water street. corner of sisson
401.289.0373 www.natporter.com
wed - sat 5 - 10p sun 5:30 - 9p open tue after labor day 5 - 10p

opened in 2004. owners/chefs: jen and nigel vincent
$$ - $$$: all major credit cards accepted
dinner. full bar. reservations recommended

warren >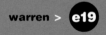

nat porter fascinates me because its young owners possess the off-the-charts confidence and verve it takes to buy a centuries-old building and transform it into one of the hippest eateries in the east bay. granted, they both worked at *the back eddy*, a renowned restaurant in westport, but still—i waitressed once, too, and i wouldn't think that would qualify me to do what jen does every night in the front of the house. thank goodness for their youth, exuberance, sensibilities, and, of course, nigel's magic grill.

imbibe:
heavenly cosmo
2004 l'hiver syrah

devour:
porter po' boys
honey dijon salmon
grilled sliced duck breast
fried calamari with linguica & smoked tomato
award-winning banana cream pie

new rivers

tiny jewel of a restaurant with a fresh, local menu
7 steeple street. corner of north main
401.751.0350 www.newriversrestaurant.com
mon - sat 5:30 - 10p

opened in 1990. owner: bruce tillinghast chef: beau vestal
$$ - $$$: all major credit cards accepted
dinner. reservations recommended

providence : college hill >

new rivers was home to my first alice waters-style eureka moment. that's when i realized that even in rhode island you can collect some lettuce from this fella's farm, a few oysters from that guy's aqua bed, and maybe find a nice free-range chicken native to tiverton. bruce puts this all together masterfully, and creates food that is uniquely and deliciously rhode island. and thank you, bruce, for providing a romantic setting to eat this magical cuisine.

imbibe:
1999 pinot noir, organic cooper mountain
1996 hermitage, paul jaboulet "la chapelle"

devour:
wild onion pâté with herbed crackers
eva's spring salad mix with poppadums
roasted red snapper on smoked shrimp rolls
crispy phyllo cup with
  strawberry-rhubarb compote

nice slice

good new york-style pizza in a college setting
267 thayer street. corner of meeting
401.453.6423 www.niceslicepizza.com
mon - sun 11a - 2a

opened in 2005. owners: al read and robert murphy
$ - $$: mc. visa
lunch. dinner. late night. first come, first served

providence > **e21**

people go to galleries to see art. me, i go to *nice slice*. for one thing, you can't eat in most art galleries. for another, *nice slice* is oozing with the work of local artists, but it's fairly under the radar. from the floor painting of the rhode island state symbol, to the silkscreened pizza boxes, to the lattice barbeque pizza itself, everything here is casually arty. eagle-eyed art enthusiasts will recognize the outline of spencer fairey's obey giant in the pizzeria's logo.

imbibe:
san benedetto sodas
aranciata

devour:
earth crisis artichoke pizza
depth-charge meatball, ricotta & pepper pizza
walkin' in the park pizza with squash & olives
something else sandwich
cranberries picnic pizza with feta & spinach

nick's on broadway

gourmet, local, fresh and neighborhoody
500 broadway. corner of tobey
401.421.0286 www.nicksonbroadway.com
tue - sat 7a - 3p & 5:30 - 10:30p sun 8a - 4p

opened in 2002. owner/chef: derek wagner
$$: all major credit cards accepted
breakfast. lunch. dinner. first come, first served

providence : west side > e22

if you, like me, can't get enough of the chef-as-rock-star notion, then *nick's* is the place for you. working the flattop, derek wagner is dazzlingly fluid in his movement—like mick with the mic used to be and he's skinny and angular, like a young david bowie. but the rock star bit ends when wagner leaves his restaurant. once off duty, you'll find him teaching cooking to kids in underprivileged neighboorhoods or bringing meals to missionaries. and oh, yeah, his food rocks, too.

imbibe:
warm cinnamon-spiced spiked apple cider
limeaid with fresh lime & spices

devour:
scottish black pearl salmon with fiddleheads
roasted long island duck with golden potatoes
asparagus & parmesan polenta with
   poached eggs
dark chocolate & smoked chile bread pudding

not just snacks

delicious, inexpensive indian food ideal for takeout

833 - 835 hope street. corner of fifth
401.831.1150
mon - sun 11a - 9p

opened in 2001. owners / chefs: mohammed and samia islam
$ - $$: all major credit cards accepted
lunch. dinner. first come, first served

providence : hope street >

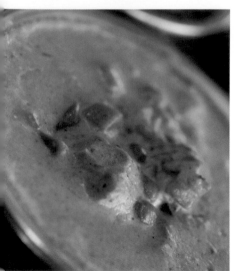

this might as well be our kitchen. not that abe and i cook anything like this, but eight times out of ten, when we're ordering takeout, *not just snacks* is where the food comes from. it's close, it's quick, and it's damn good. further, having shot all my tastebuds years ago in a habanero hush puppy eating contest, i am happy to report that this place knows how to make things spicy enough to register. spicy enough that i came here when my second labor was tardy and then delivered within the day. there could not be less décor, but it's what's in the pots, not on the walls, that matters.

imbibe:
mango lassi
indian soda

devour:
bhindi masala
chicken tandoori
vegetable biryani
malai kofta
idli sambhar

olga's cup and saucer

tasty breakfast and lunch in a garden setting
103 point street. corner of richmond
401.831.6666
mon - fri b7a - 4p sat 8a - 4p

opened in 1997. owners: olga bravo and rebecca wagner
$$: mc. visa
breakfast. lunch. brunch. treats. first come, first served

providence : downcity >

olga's cup and saucer just screams tranquility. wait—that doesn't make sense. it whispers tranquility. when deadlines loom, and my nerves are frayed and i'm looking for a bit of calm, this sheltering garden is where i go to hide from the madding crowd. so do scores of others, but that's just fine with me. we're all here to relax and enjoy the artistry coming out of olga and rebecca's kitchen.

imbibe:
ginger lemonade
lattes & capuccinos

devour:
shrimp pad thai
cuban sandwich
pane francese
strawberry turnover
black-and-white layer cake

pastiche fine desserts

scratch bakery items made with care and quality ingredients

92 spruce street. corner of dean
401.861.5190 www.pastichefinedesserts.com
tue - thu 8:30a - 11p fri - sat 8:30a - 11:30p sun 10a - 10p

opened in 1989. owners: brandt heckert and eileen collins
$$: all major credit cards accepted
coffee. treats. first come, first served

providence : federal hill >

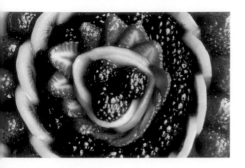

when i was huge with my first daughter, i had one of those insane pregnancy epiphanies: i would learn to make really fine, really exquisite, special-occasion cakes. then whenever an occasion arose, i would have something to contribute that spoke of love, effort and skill. this worked great when i had one kid. less so, when i had two. by the time i had three, i realized it was beaucoup easier and just as rewarding to go up to the hill and get one of *pastiche's* exquisite cakes instead.

imbibe:
strong espressos
creamy cappucinos

devour:
mascapone torte
white chocolate orange torte
banana cream tart
fresh fruit tart
apricot almond chiffon

Blondies
w/ walnuts, white &
dark chunk
$1.25 each

persimmon

seasonal, sophisticated food in a winsome little restaurant

31 state street. between thames and hope
401.254.7474 www.persimmonbristol.com
tue - sun 5 - 9:30p

opened in 2005. owner/chef: champe speidel
$$ - $$$: all major credit cards accepted
dinner. full bar. reservations recommended

bristol >

back in the day, i used to eat at *gracie's* on atwells. for no explicable reason, i felt an odd closeness to this little restaurant and its talented chef, champe. that's the power of good food, i guess. when champe left, i kept an ear out for his next venture. then rumors of *persimmon* began to circulate, and i could not get there soon enough. of course, champe did not disappoint. drop whatever you're doing and go.

imbibe:
westport rivers rjr sparkling wine

devour:
the persimmon cheese experience
yellow watermelon & sheeps' milk feta salad
butter basted lobster carnaroli risotto
crispy skin massachusetts black bass filet
  with a ragout of parmesan gnocchi

puerini's

northern italian featuring handmade pasta and a warm ambience

24 memorial boulevard. corner of bellevue

401.847.5506

mon - thu 5 - 10p fri - sat 5 - 11p sun 5 - 9p

opened in 1982. owner: dan puerini chef: christopher jones

$$ - $$$: all major credit cards accepted

dinner. late night. full bar. first come, first served

newport >

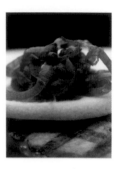

puerini's is a special place. the pasta is fresh, hand-made by the family, and has that wonderful flavor and mouthfeel that sets it apart from the usual. the decor is simple, warm and mellow, featuring black and white pictures snapped in Italy. the preparations are tasty and pleasing to the eye. you can be rowdy at the downstairs bar or immersed in your conversation in one of the upstairs enclaves. puerini's is now required dining when i'm in newport.

imbibe:
santa margherita pinot grigio 2005
cesari amaronei 2001

devour:
pasta con salsicce
melanzane eggplant
homemade polenta
pollo alla marsala
calamari e gamberetti with linguini

red fez lodge & lounge

delicious food in a quirky environment
49 peck street. between friendship and pine
401.272.1212
tue - wed 5 - 11p thu - sat 5p - 12a bar tue - thu until 1a fri - sat until 2a

opened in 2001. owners: sara kilguss and edward reposa chef: edward reposa
$$: all major credit cards accepted
dinner. late night. full bar. first come, first served

providence : downcity >

i'm pretty sure you've been to *red fez*. it's that cool place with the fun, irreverent décor and the innovative, larky menu. you know the one. it's that place that makes you wish you had a bigger vintage store budget and a better eye for the off-kilter. chances are, you went there for dinner and ended up in the bar—excuse me, the lodge. and before you knew it, it was last call. if somehow you haven't been to *red fez*—it's time.

imbibe:
thee gingered gentleman
narragansett lager

devour:
roasted corn & chourico stuffies
pulled chicken sandwich with cumin slaw
grilled wild striped bass
watermelon, feta & mint salad with lime
pear & ginger cobbler

red stripe

a high-energy american brasserie

465 angell street. corner of elmgrove

401.437.6950

lunch mon - sat 11:30a - 5p sun 9a - 4p dinner mon - sat 5 - 11p sun 4 - 10p

bar open until 1a

opened in 2005. owner: jaime d'oliveira chef: terrence maul

$$ - $$$: all major credit cards accepted

lunch. dinner. brunch. full bar. reservations recommended

providence : wayland square >

my first time to *red stripe*, one word came to mind: din. *red stripe* reminded me more of a new york city restaurant than any i'd ever been to in providence. i consider this a good thing. *red stripe* has a buzz and an electricity that i think makes everything taste better. not everyone considers noise a bonus, however. to them, i say, wear earplugs and go instead for the frites with aioli.

imbibe:
red stripe bloody mary
sakonnet gewurztraminer

devour:
trio of homemade deviled eggs
portuguese moules frites
grilled shrimp & avocado parfait
smoked pork tenderloin
mango cheesecake with kiwi

revival house cafe

good food plus good movies

42-46 high street. corner of canal street
401.315.2770 www.revivalhouse.net
tue - sun noon - 10p open mon during the summer

opened in 2003. owners: emily steffian and daniel kemil
$: mc. visa
lunch. dinner. wine bar. first come, first served

westerly >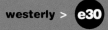

a good movie paired with good food has a reese's like rightness to it. however, for whatever reason, this concept hasn't really caught on in rhode island much. at *revival house cafe*, emily and dan have nailed it. they have an eye for detail and a quirkiness that extends from the vintage library card wallpaper in the restroom to the hilarious selection of postcards in the lobby. plus, they keep halloumi in their deli case. siskel would have come for the movie; ebert the food.

imbibe:
the best fruity sangria
fizzy lizzy sparkling sodas

devour:
turkey brie & baby spinach panini
halloumi, tomato & basil salad
old lyme white cheddar popcorn
lemon sorbet served in a lemon
chocolate covered cranberries

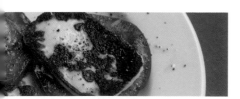

61

roba dolce

authentic gelato in an italian street cafe atmosphere

450 thames street. corner of howard
401.848.9600 www.robadolce.com
mon - thu 9a - 9:30p fri - sat 9a - 11p sun 9a - 9p

opened in 2005. owner: matthew olerio chef: matthew hewitt
$ - $$: all major credit cards accepted
breakfast. lunch. dinner. first come, first served

newport > **e31**

i scream for gelato. for *roba dolce's* melon gelato, i'll shriek. caterwaul. ululate. whatever it takes. the offerings at *roba dolce* taste delicious, but for the visually oriented, the added bonus is that there are lots of really cute italian guys on staff. and on newport's thames street, with its sidewalk tables and black-clad employees, *roba dolce* actually feels a little bit like italy. tastes like it, too.

imbibe:
the roba dolce: iced cappuccino with gelato
chocolate federal hill frappe

devour:
pink grapefruit sorbetto
panna cotta gelato
pistachio cannoli
egg, bacon & chedder breakfast panini
ultimate grilled cheese panini

salvation café

festive dining and drinking, tiki-style

140 broadway. corner of ayrault
401.847.2620 www.salvationcafe.com
mon - sun 5p - midnight

opened in 1993. owners: susan lamond and bill stark
$$: all major credit cards
dinner. full bar. first come, first served

newport > **e32**

i credit *salvation café* with actually drawing my husband and me to rhode island. on our first scouting trip, we overshot providence, kind of on purpose, because it looked small compared to new york (duh). we drove on to newport and, with our future in the balance, ate a meal while weighing new york or rhode island. rhode island or new york? it all came down to our experience at *salvation café*. we stayed. one house, three kids, and two satisfying careers later, we say salvation indeed.

imbibe:
pitcher of sangria
coconut mojito

devour:
seared red snapper with carmelized leeks
jerk chicken with sweet potato shrimp tamales
chicken tikka
fennel salad
chocolate banana purses

seven stars bakery

scratch breads and pastries from the best ingredients

820 hope street. corner of fourth
401.521.2200 www.sevenstarsbakery.com
mon - fri 6:30a - 6p sat - sun 7a - 4p

opened in 2001. owner / chefs: lynn and jim williams
$$: all major credit cards accepted
breakfast. lunch. treats. first come, first served

providence : hope street >

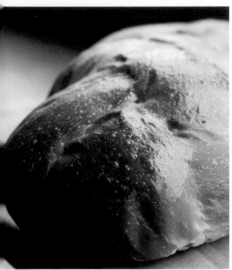

remember flash mobs? somebody would issue an email telling everybody to gather, often for no discernable purpose. that's what *seven stars* reminds me of. one day in 2001 everybody suddenly congregated at a bakery on the site of a former gas station. where did they come from? where had they been? who knows. flash mobs may be a footnote, but *seven stars* still goes strong drawing families from near and far whose purpose is clear—to enjoy the most delicious, artisanal bread, iced coffee with coffee ice cubes, and neighborhood conviviality.

imbibe:
iced new harvest coffee with coffee ice cubes
sid wainer fresh-squeezed juices

devour:
chocolate almond croissant
spinach & cheese calzone
ginger bread muffins
sticky bun with toasted pecans
durum stick with butter

slice of heaven

wholesome variety of all-day fare

32 narragansett avenue. corner of coronado

401.423.9866

mon - tue 6a - 3p wed - sun 6a - 9p

opened in 2001. chef / owners: steven and maria liebhauser

$ - $$: mc. visa

breakfast. lunch. dinner. brunch. first come, first served

jamestown >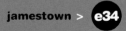

evenings spent at my friend anna's nearby summer home require mornings spent at *slice of heaven*. the oatmeal there, when accompanied by a huge cup of coffee, seems like it will offer enough energy to propel you through the whole day. if it does eventually wear off, that's perfectly okay, though, because then you can just return for lunch and since we're on vacation a champagne cocktail is called for.

imbibe:
frozen hot chocolate
champagne cocktails

devour:
hearty oatmeal
thai curried shrimp with udon noodles
roast beef agro e dolce
california turkey club sandwich
strawberry shortcake

stanley's famous hamburgers

old-timey burger joint

535 dexter street. corner of rand
401.726.9689 www.stanleyshamburgers.com
mon - thu 11a - 8p fri 11a - 10p sat 11a - 9p

opened in 1932. owner: gregory raheb
$ - $$: all major credit cards accepted
lunch. dinner. first come, first served

pawtucket/central falls > **e35**

get a load of the facade at this place. vibrant, bold red neon yells *stanley's*. i'm like a magpie; i can't say no to shiny bright things, so this is one of the first restaurants i visited when i moved to rhode island. i come back over and over because i can't get enough of those crazy, gravy-and-cheese soaked fries. sure the burgers are swell and as noted in the name, famous, but give me the fries.

imbibe:
root beer float
strawberry shake

devour:
quebec-style fries with mozzarella & gravy
stanleyburger
fried clam strip plate
delmonico shaved steak on a torpedo roll
housemade chili

sun and moon

genuine home-cooked korean
95 warren avenue. corner of fifth
401.435.0214
tue - sat 11:30a - 10:00p sun 11:30a - 9:00p

opened in 2002. owner/chef: il-sun jeon
$ - $$: all major credit cards accepted
lunch. dinner. wine bar. first come, first served

east providence > **e36**

i love asian food, and i make one small demand of purveyors: choose a country. variety is lovely in shoes, say, but less appealing when a menu spans an entire hemisphere. that's why i was beside myself with happiness when *sun and moon* materialized one day. korean food. that's it. bi bim bop with its signature crunchy bottom in stone pots. short ribs with a sweet, intense glaze. in the small space wedged next to a tattoo shop, chef il-sun jeon makes everything on demand and keeps it simple and delicious.

imbibe:
hot green tea
korean rice punch

devour:
dolshot bi bim bop
korean barbeque
fried dumplings with vegetables
sweet potato noodles with rice

taqueria lupita

small, family-run mexican restaurant with big flavors

765 dexter street. corner of cowden
401.724.2650
tue - thu 11a - 9p fri - sat 11a - 10p sun 11a - 8p

opened in 2002. owners: bertina and eladio ramos chef: bertina ramos
$: all major credit cards accepted
lunch. dinner. first come, first served

pawtucket/central falls > **e37**

we lamented for years that we couldn't get good mexican food around providence. originally, we were brought out to central falls to try a neighboring restaurant. it was fine and very cheap, but it didn't quite make the grade. then *taqueria lupita* opened and we lament no more. in fact, we rejoice now because of "working mom" bertina's complex, flavorful and authentic meals. the ramoses, originally from puebla, have brought the real deal to our little corner of the world.

imbibe:
mango batidos
atole de sabores

devour:
camarones enchipotlados
cheese tostada
chips with red & green salsa
chicken enchilada with mole
flan

taqueria pacifica

high quality taco stand in an art incubator
105 empire street. between washington and westminster
401.621.8785
tue - sat noon - 10p

opened in 2006. owner: allison kyner chef: tyler long
$ - $$: mc. visa
lunch. dinner. saturday brunch. full bar. first come, first served

providence : downcity >

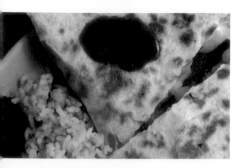

first there was the truck. or "781-truk" to be exact. that was the number to call if you wanted to find out where *taqueria pacifica* was serving fantastic mexican-style street food that night. now i don't have to call when i need my fish taco fix. i just amble on down to downcity and take one of those sweet, diagonal parking spaces in front of *as220*. there allison and tyler are still cranking out fresh, cheap eats, but now in the midst of one of providence's most energetic art scenes.

imbibe:
pacifica's horchata
freshly squeezed limeaid

devour:
osita burrito
fish taco
shrimp quesadilla
joesadilla
burrito deluxe

the hot club

waterfront bar

575 s water street. corner of point
401.861.9007 www.thenetmill.com/hotclub
sun - thu noon - 1a fri - sat noon - 2a

opened in 1983. owners: tom bates and josh miller
$: all major credit cards accepted
lunch. dinner. late night. full bar. first come, first served

providence : wickenden street >

you don't have to ride a harley to hang here, although it's a common accessory for the night crowd. but in a case of multiple personalities, during the daytime *the hot club* is filled with all kinds. after all both bikers and bankers (maybe some are both) can appreciate a waterfront locale that has stunning architectural views of the power plant and the city. also appreciated by all are the potent drinks and not-too-fussy, goes down good with a beer, food.

imbibe:
custom made cocktails
imported beers & ales

devour:
chilidog with saugy weiners
chicken on a stick
grilled zucchini
grilled chiliburger
chicken salad sandwich

79

tio mateo's

simple, healthy mexican
537 main street. corner of cvs plaza
401.886.1973 www.tiomateos.com
mon - thu 11a - 8p fri - sat 11a - 9p

opened in 2005. owner/chef: matt wronski
$ - $$: mc. visa
lunch. dinner. first come, first served

east greenwich > e40

i think mole sauce is the single greatest culinary feat. a spicy, savory chocolate sauce. how could that possibly be improved on? left to my own devices, i might just layer mole over mole and call that a meal. fortunately for my balanced diet, the fine chefs at *tio mateo* provide a simple and tasty menu of burritos, enchiladas and tacos over which to spread the liquid gold.

imbibe:
no-alcohol senorial sangria soda
yes-alcohol sangria by the pitcher

devour:
burrito del mar
ensalada mama dana
albondigas soup with meatballs
shrimp diablo
el mateo supremo burrito with mole sauce

trattoria simpatico

creative american with european flair near the bay

13 narragansett avenue. corner of conanicus
401.423.3731 www.trattoriasimpatico.com
sun - wed noon - 10p thu - sat noon - 11p (appetizers only 3 - 5p)

opened in 1993. owner: phyllis bedard   chef: kevin gaudreau
$$ - $$$: all major credit cards accepted
lunch. dinner. full bar. reservations recommended

jamestown > **e41**

if i were a' courting again *trattoria simpatico* is the place i would want to be taken to by potential suitors. outoors under the twinkly lights and the silk lanterns is ripe for romance while enjoying the fresh breezes from nearby narragansett bay. and dining on oysters and other gifts from the sea is sure to get the heart a' pounding. my courting days may be over, but i can still appreciate this restaurant for its many charms.

imbibe:
negroni with campari & bitters
copper beech martini

devour:
green curry prince edward isles mussels
pemaquid oysters
roasted corn pancetta & clam chowder
george's bank scallops with leeks
rack of lamb with chard & potato crisps

tucker's bistro

bistro-style dining in an art-filled environment
150 broadway. corner of ayrault
401.846.3449 www.tuckersbistro.com
mon - sun 6 - 10p

opened in 1995. owner: tucker harris chef: peter hand
$$ - $$$: all major credit cards accepted
dinner. full bar. reservations recommended

newport >

a diner at *tucker's bistro* once called it a cross between an art gallery, a library and a bordello. this pleased tucker himself no end. i can honestly call this place "eclectic" and not feel like i've had to fall back on some overused word. it is equal parts romantic and whimsical. i could go there with my husband or a gaggle of girls, and either way, feel like i was in the right spot.

imbibe:
sassy cinnotti
meursault labouré-roi 2001 burgundy

devour:
house-smoked duck breast with rainbow chard
pan-seared scallops with sweet pea risotto
thai shrimp nachos
jonah lump crab cakes with citrus aioli
molten chocolate cake

85

vintage

modern new american in old milltown setting

4 s main street. corner of bernon
401.765.1234 www.vintageri.com
lunch mon - fri 11:30a - 2p dinner sun - thu 5 - 9p fri - sat 5 - 10p

opened in 2006. owner: larry lovejoy chef: brian counihan
$$ - $$$: all major credit cards accepted
lunch. dinner. full bar. reservations recommended

woonsocket >

yowza! props to the owner of *vintage* who has created an urbane looking restaurant in a city some call "blue collar." and still more props for bringing along a chef who will draw out the foodies from neighboring communities. and the most props of all for mastering the simple gin martini, an art often lost these days but here skillfully rendered. this is a destination restaurant worth the trip.

imbibe:
dry gin tanqueray martini with a twist
ginger margarita with fresh ginger & lime

devour:
crispy olive crusted #1 tuna
truffled parmesan hash browns
black angus bone-in rib eye
pan crisp west coast halibut
salmon lumi with avocado & crispy wontons

white electric coffee

art, coffee, food and community
711 westminster street. corner of dean
401.453.3007
mon - fri 7a - 6:30p sat 8a - 6:30p sun 9a - 4p

opened in 2000. owners: jed arkley and tonya langford
$ - $$: cash
breakfast. lunch. first come, first served

providence : west side >

first, you have to love the name *white electric coffee*. it belonged to a repair shop in the coffee house's original location. who doesn't want their coffee... electric!? then there's the buzz generated by the community who've made *white electric* the unofficial hq of the west side arts and culture scene. finally, there's the curvy walls of happenings, always papered with the neighborhood and the city's most interesting events.

imbibe:
italian soda
espresso macchiato

devour:
oatmeal with steamed milk & honey
chedder & pesto sandwich
ham & cheese sandwich
bagel with tofutti cream cheese
white electric salad

xo steakhouse

a sassy steakhouse

125 n main street. corner of meeting
401.273.9090 www.xosteakhouse.com
sun - thu 5 - 10p bar until 1am fri - sat 5-11p bar until 2am

opened in 1997. owners: john elkhay, rick and cheryl bready chef: ben lloyd
$$ - $$$: all major credit cards accepted
dinner. full bar. reservations recommended

providence : college hill > e45

A dry lentil, a fertile year.
scottish proverb

i have nothing but hugs and kisses for this lively restaurant. *xo steakhouse* has got a whimsy that doesn't sink to gimmicky. you just have to love a place that urges you to eat your dessert first. i haven't actually done that yet, because that would mean delaying my opportunity to devour the xo filet with seared scallops. don't get me wrong, crème brûée is great in general, and it's fantastic here, but i have to give my love to the surf & turf right now.

imbibe:
pomegranate martini
espresso martini

devour:
xo filet with seared scallops & aspargus
grilled tuna miso with pomegranate puree
rhode island calamari
crème brûlée sampler

about eat.shop

the first thing to know about the *eat.shop guides* is that they are the only guides dedicated to just eating and shopping. okay, we list some hotels, because we know that you need to sleep. and don't forget to whittle out some time for cultural activities—all of the businesses featured in the book are helmed by creative types who are highly influenced by the arts and sights of the cities they live in—culture is good for you.

the *eat.shop guides* feature approximately 90 carefully picked businesses, all of them homegrown and distinctive. some are small and some are big. some are posh and some are street. some are spendy and some require nothing more than pocket change. some are old school and some are shiny and new. some are hip and some are under-the-radar. point being, we like to feature a mix of places that are unique because you can feel the passionate vision of the owner(s) from the moment you step through their door, eat their food, touch their wares.

the guides each have one author. these authors have diverse backgrounds ranging from a graphic designer to a fashion stylist to a radio talk show host. each has the unique talent to research, write and photograph—which gives their book a distinctive voice and visual style. and a note on the photographs, they are shot with natural light and there is no propping or styling used—so what you see is the real deal. as for the copy, you already know we love these places because they're in the book, so we're not offering reviews or critiques or marketing blah blah. instead you get our experiential mini-stories.

enough explaining, here are a couple of things to remember when using this guide: remember that hours change seasonally, so always call or check the website before you go. we apologize if a featured business has closed—being small and local can be a rough road and some businesses don't make it—so use this book often and support the locals, they are the soul of the city. remember that items mentioned or pictures shown may not be available any longer, but there will most definitely be something even more fantastic available. finally, each guide has a two-year life span, and each new edition is different than the last—so collect them all! and if you don't have the past editions, not to worry. every business that has ever been featured in an *eat.shop guide* is archived on our website.

eat! shop! enjoy!

kaie wellman
creator and publisher of the *eat.shop guides*

jan's notes on rhode island

i'm pretty much a real rhode islander now. my family hasn't been here for centuries, the true standard, but i can now enjoy the occasional gagger. i can also offer directions based on where things used to be. and i gave birth to a daughter at women & infants while blossom dearie breathed out the song *you come from rhode island*.

it wasn't always this way. i settled here rather suddenly one winter and realized i had two choices: think of myself as someone just passing through or jump in and embrace my new state. i chose to jump and that decision has been richly rewarded ever since.

back then, i had a set of unusual and complementary circumstances. i was deeply curious about the ocean state, was not seeking a job, knew almost nobody and was trying to furnish my first home. i had long days to drive alone along major roads, wooded routes, and neighborhood cul-de-sacs. whenever something caught my eye, i would pop in—surveying the offerings on display, tasting the specialties of the house and generally amusing myself by uncovering many of the fascinating, idiosyncratic and notable treasures of my new state. it was a wonderful research period for what would become this book. nothing beats that kind of meandering exploration, and if you find yourself with that kind of free time, i say it's well worth it.

however, as noted, few people have that kind of time. for the rest of you, i offer this book as a handy and hardy field guide to some of the most "stylishly unique" places the state has to offer. i've distilled the impressive variety into 87 of my favorite shops and restaurants. it's by no means comprehensive, but then, what's the fun in that? i'm acting as a filter and a friend, sharing my thoughts about what i think makes a place stand out.

take this book along with you. where possible, we've provided maps for some of the more concentrated neighborhoods to help you find your way. in others, your on your own, but i know you're resourceful like that. and by all means, when you find places you think embody the *eat.shop* style, please return the favor and let me know!

jan faust
jan@eatshopguides.com
july 2006

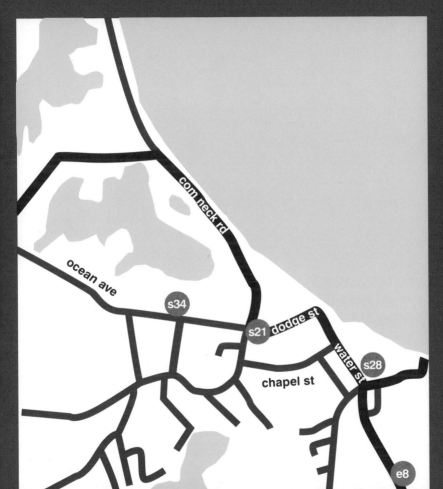

eat

e8 > hotel manisses

shop

s21 > lazy fish
s28 > pelle nuda
s34 > shoreline

com neck rd

ocean ave

s34

s21 dodge st

water st

s28

chapel st

e8

note: all maps face north

block island

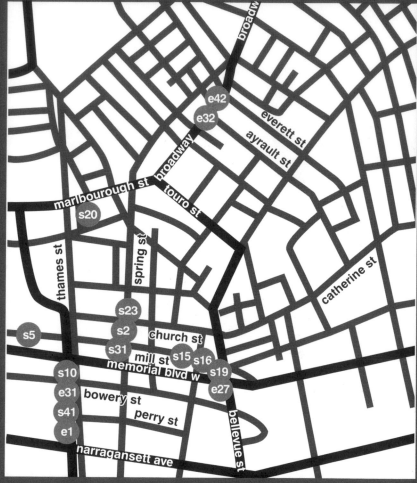

eat

shop

note: all maps face north

newport

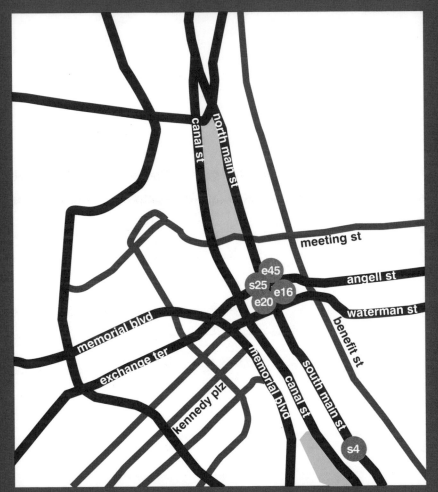

eat

e16 > mill's tavern
e20 > new rivers
e45 > xo steakhouse

shop

s4 > capucine
s25 > martina & compan

note: all maps face north

providence : college hill

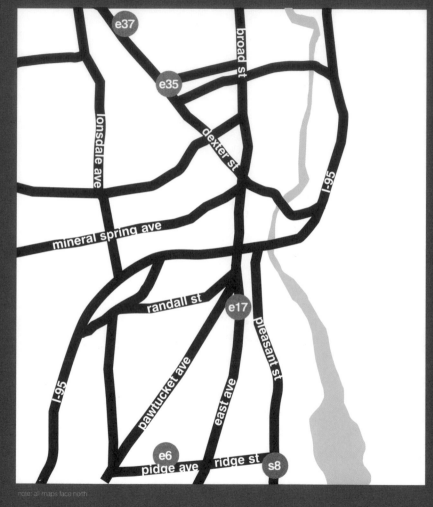

eat

e6 > garden grille
e17 > modern diner
e35 > stanley's
famous hamburgers
e37 > taqueria lupita

shop

s8 > east side eden

note: all maps face north

pawtucket / central falls

note: all maps face north

providence : downcity

eat

e24 > olga's cup and saucer
e28 > red fez lodge & lounge
e38 > taqueria pacifica

shop

s3 > butterfield
s22 > lily pad

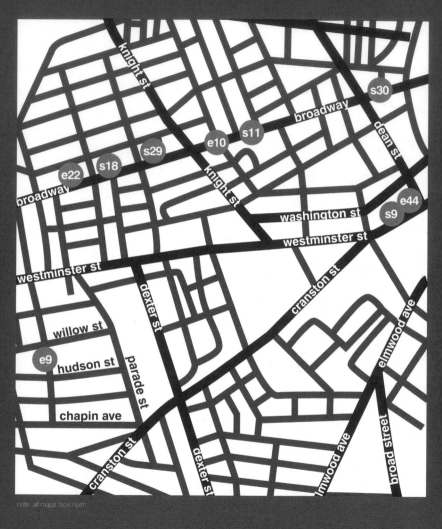

note: all maps face north

providence : west side

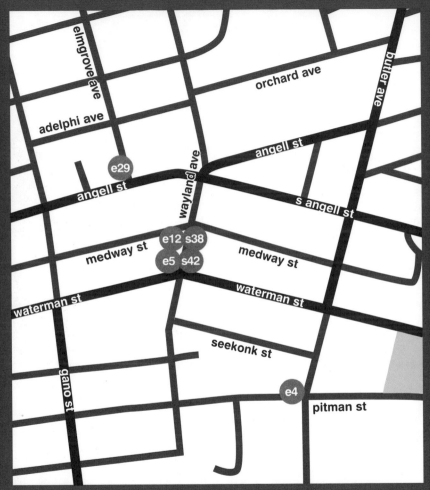

eat

e4 > eastside
marketplace
e5 > farmstead
e12 > la laiterie
e29 > red stripe

shop

s38 > strada
s42 > wendy
brown linens

note: all maps face north

providence: wayland square

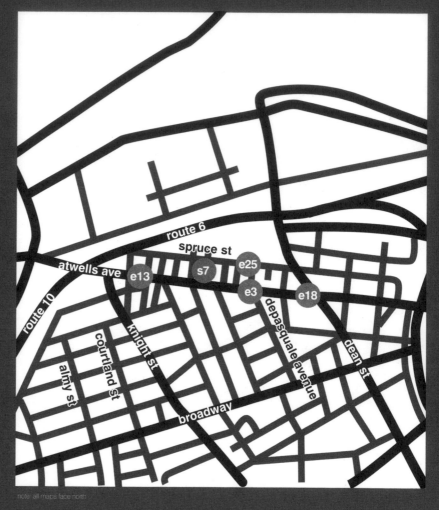

route 6

spruce st

atwells ave

e13

s7

e25

e3

e18

route 10

depasquale avenue

dean st

knight st

courtland st

almy st

broadway

note: all maps face north

providence: federal hill

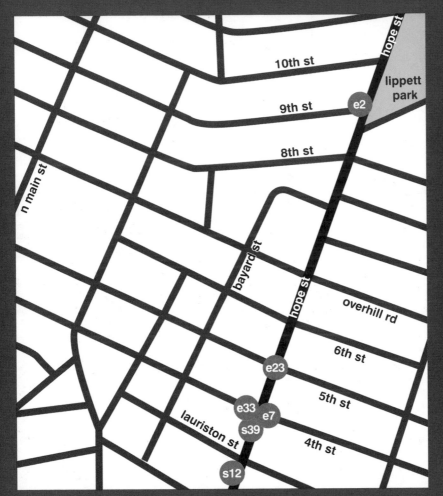

eat

e2 > chez pascal
e7 > garrison confection
e23 > not just snacks
e33 > seven stars bakery

shop

s12 > frog and toad
s39 > studio hop

note: all maps face north

providence : hope street

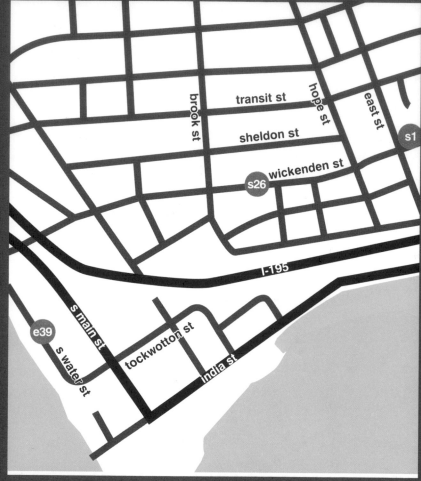

eat

e39 > the hot club

shop

s1 > acme antiques
s26 > mignonette

transit st

brook st

hope st

east st

s1

sheldon st

wickenden st

s26

I-195

e39

s main st

tockwotton st

s water st

india st

note: all maps face north

providence : wickenden

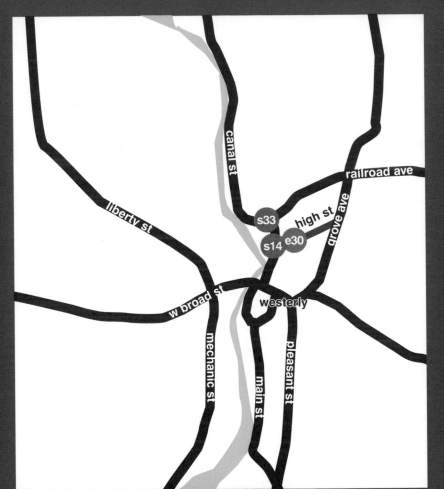

eat

e30 > revival house cafe

shop

s14 > hammen home
s33 > 7 ply

note: all maps face north

westerly

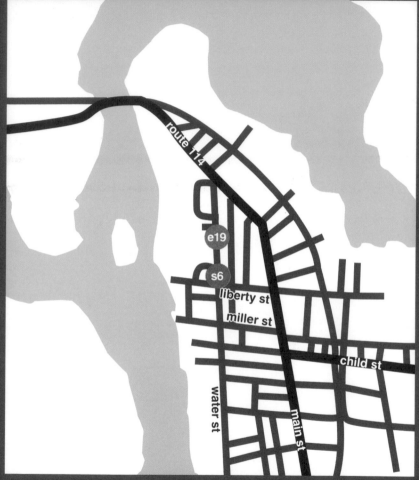

eat

e19 > nat porter

shop

s6 > dish

route 114

e19

s6

liberty st

miller st

child st

water st

main st

note: all maps face north

warren

jan's twenty favorite places

eat

1 > new rivers

2 > julian's

3 > la laiterie

4 > lili marlene's

5 > revival house

6 > nat porter

7 > tacqueria lupita

8 > persimmon

9 > not just snacks

10 > sun and moon

shop

11 > alloy

12 > cathers & coyne

13 > simple pleasures

14 > lazy fish

15 > mignonette

16 > trappings

17 > dish

18 > diva's palace

19 > figments

20 > roy

where to lay your weary head

there's many great places to stay in rhode island, but here's a couple of my picks:

castle inn hotel
590 ocean drive. newport
888.466.1355
www.castlehillinn.com
$409 - $989

mill street inn
75 mill street. newport
401.849.9500 / 800.392.1316
www.millstreetinn.com
$299 - $399

hotel providence
311 westminster street. providence
401.861.8000
www.thehotelprovidence.com
$200 - $229

the providence biltmore
11 dorrance street. providence
401.421.0700
www.providencebiltmore.com
$169 - $189

the providence westin
one west exchange street. providence
401.598.8000
www.westinprovidence.com
$199 - $319

acme antiques

art nouveau through '70s retro home furnishings
460 wickenden street. corner of governor
401.374.2394
fri - sat noon - 5p or by appointment or chance

opened in 1998. owners: kevin regan and kurt smith
mc. visa. amex
prop rentals. styling

providence : wickenden street > **s1**

acme owner kevin and i both came from brooklyn to providence about eight years ago. he didn't mean to come here necessarily but kept bringing mid-century pieces from williamsburg up to his friend's shop where the items were quickly snatched up. somehow, those weekly trips evolved into kevin's moving here, which is a good thing for providence and a great thing for my house.

covet:
'50s pop swivel chair inspired by
   vladmir kagen
heywood wakefield dogbone chairs
space-age smoked lucite dining set
italian colored glass vases
melmac dinnerware set by russel wright
1923 venetian handblown chandelier
deco through '50s white pottery vases

alloy gallery

a little store of modern jewelry treasures

160 spring street. corner of mill
800.959.2977 or 401.619.2265 www.alloygallery.com
mon - sun noon - 6p varies seasonally

opened in 2005. owner: tamar kern
all major credit cards accepted
made to order

newport > **s2**

i got lost in newport looking for a store and stumbled into *alloy*, which turned out to be quite possibly my best-ever serendipitous find. inside the narrow, spare shop, you'll discover work by eight or ten designers, mostly risd graduates. each tall case features deeply original work gleaming in silvers and golds but also featuring enamels, wools, and other fun materials. don't wait to get lost to find it yourself. it's on spring street. go.

covet:
heather guidero flocked sprout earrings
sara dunbar rhodes fan-shaped earrings
tamar kern seed pearl pod 18k gold earrings
jenn parnell enamel & pearl necklace
tamar kern stackable cone rings
islay taylor fleur-de-lis earrings
seung-hea lee necklace

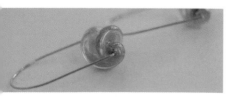

butterfield

high-end, loft-feeling home furnishings store

232 westminster street. corner of union
401.273.3331 www.butterfieldprovidence.com
tue - fri 11a - 6p sat 10a - 6p sun noon - 5p

opened in 2005. owner: mindy matouk
all major credit cards accepted
interior design advice and casual consultation

providence : downcity > **s3**

walk down westminster street, and you're in providence. step into *butterfield*, and you're in manhattan. or so it feels, at this luscious, brick loft-style store in downcity. owner mindy has tapped into all that is right with city living at this luscious, airy, loft-style store on westminster street. if you've asked yourself, 'how will providence furnish this giant condo craze it's undergoing?' *butterfield* is part of your answer. or perhaps, you've asked yourself, 'how would I look draped across a kiwi green ultrasuede sofa.' again, *butterfield* would be your answer.

covet:
mitchell & gold ultrasuede chair
chilewich place mats
john derian decoupage plates
robert abbey gourd lamps
jonathan adler specs case
renata woven necklaces
swedish summer soap

capucine

clothing boutique with feminine appeal

359 s main. corner of james
401.273.6622
mon - fri 11a - 6p sat 11a - 5p

opened in 2002. owner: heidi branley-keller
all major credit cards accepted

providence : college hill > **s4**

this is my go-to store when i need just one item to elevate a ho-hum outfit into something that sizzles. maybe i'll select one of the spunky t's to layer under a jacket or a sassy halter to pair with jeans. different stores cause me to shop in different ways, and *capucine* is one where i slow down and choose carefully. it's a quality over quantity thing. and that's a good thing.

covet:
milly plunge neck halter top
white & warren cashmere wrap
jill stuart camisole
tyler malibu bags & belts
tory burch velvet dressy t's
twelfth street by cynthia vincent sweaters
lacoste long-sleeved shirts

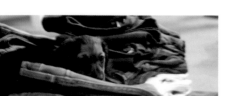

cathers & coyne

hot shoes for cool people
18 bowen's wharf. off of thames street
401.849.5757 www.hotshoesforcoolpeople.com
mon - thu 10a - 10p fri - sat 10a - 11p sun 11a - 8p

opened in 2002. owners: jake cathers and stephen coyne
all major credit cards accepted
online shopping. made to order

newport > **s5**

did somebody say shoes? somewhere in the world, somebody just said shoes. my highly attuned ears heard it. i'm pretty sure that when jake and steve opened their shop in newport, i felt a small temblor all the way over in pawtucket. this shoe store rates high on the shoe richter scale for me. in fact, if this store were a shoe emergency alert, it would be code red. oh, there it was again. somebody else just said shoes. i hope whoever it was has the good sense to go to *cathers & coyne*.

covet:
linda pritcher silkscreen leather wedge mules
morenatom ribboned pleated heels
penny loves kenny crinkle patent sandal
cocobelle m.o.p. leather thong
terre peck italian flat
think euro casual thong sandal
barry & boyle zipper-front tank

117

dish

beautiful clothes & jewelry

155 water street. corner of company street
401.247.7705 www.dishri.com
tue - sat 11a - 5:30p sun noon - 5p

opened in 2003. owners: keri cronin and sara volino
all major credit cards accepted

warren >

dish taps into many of my preferences and peculiarities. i love one word store names. got that covered at *dish*. i fantasize about the mother-daughter owned shop. *dish* has that too with sara and keri. and then there's the style put forth by these two proprietresses—a thrilling mélange of local and worldly. the location is practically waterfront, another plus. and finally, the sales. the sale rack is steeply discounted and always changing. there's just nothing to dis at *dish*.

covet:
julez rose gold necklace
skirtz skirt
amet & ladue scarves
japanese exfoliating towels
utility striped skirts
philippa kunisch earrings
aster & sage cellphone clutch

diva's palace

some vintage, more new, all stylish
299 atwells avenue. corner of sutton
401.831.0148
mon - wed 11a - 5p thu - fri 11a - 8p sat 10a - 9p sun noon - 5p

opened in 1992. owners: michael and joanne turner
all major credit cards accepted
alterations/tailoring. made to order. personal shopping

providence : federal hill > **s7**

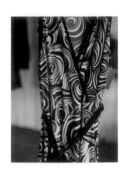

once upon a time, michael had *diva's palace* at pontiac mills and it was pure heaven for me. when it closed, i felt that the one local outlet for truly curated vintage wear was lost forever. then, what's this? *diva's palace* on atwells? it is reborn, but with a twist: michael now applies his admiration of bygone fashion to new clothes which he designs for his own label. and sprinkled among tailored victorian jackets and reconstructed hats are other quality brands and other worthy vintage. now heaven's on the hill.

covet:
diva's palace victorian street jacket
joyce flared jeans
so cool pucci style print dress
reconstructed hats
voxx tuxedo t-shirt dress
final touch dress
hand-tailored restyled vintage fur coats

east side eden

essentials for the urban gardener
1 alfred stone. corner of pleasant
401.726.2700 www.eastsideeden.com
mon, wed - sat 10a - 5p sun noon - 5p

opened in 2004. owners: alexandra knott and christopher burke
all major credit cards accepted

pawtucket / central falls > **s8**

alex, the owner of *east side eden* is one of those people you buy a trinket from, and then next thing you know she's coming to your parties. she's outgoing, personable and operates her store like an extension of her house. if her house is anything like the store, it's one helluva house. *east side eden* features a giant greenhouse always chockablock with thriving plants, outdoor furnishings and accessories. inside, in the historic cottage, she keeps the small, delicate things she describes as "yummy hostess gifts." if i do visit her house, i'll be sure to bring one.

covet:
vietnamese women's co-op stoles
alex's handstuffed toile bags of
   worm castings (or, poop)
bougies la francaise chlorophylle candles
janet white concrete bird feeders
southside community landtrust herbal teas
8 women fish emulsion fertilizer
ceramic cookware from columbia

figments

high quality stationery and other finds
717 westminster street. corner of dean
401.588.5180 www.figmentsdesign.com
tue 11a - 5p wed - sat 11a - 5:30p sun - mon by appointment

opened in 2004. owner: peggy lo
mc. visa
online shopping

providence : west side > **s9**

i love the smell of paper in the morning—and all day long, really—especially when it's letterpressed, silk-screened, etched, engraved or marked by any other creative method through which design is transferred onto pulped fibers. at *figments*, there are beautiful papers, cards, notes and wrapping accessories everywhere. but it doesn't stop there. peggy has an acute eye for beautiful and interesting items beyond the paper goods—which makes for an alluring shopping experience.

covet:
roost decorated piglets
barbara schriber cards
lily wang fingerless gloves
neisha crossland papers
sesame letterpress coasters
sukie hankie
aranzi aronzo screen-printed pouch

fountain spa & boutique

wide assortment of bath and beauty products

400 thames street. corner of ann
401.324.6060 www.fountainspaboutique.com
mon - tue 11a - 7p sat 11a - 10p sun noon - 6p

opened in 2003. owners: robert rotondo jr. and rebecca warren
all major credit cards accepted

newport >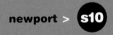

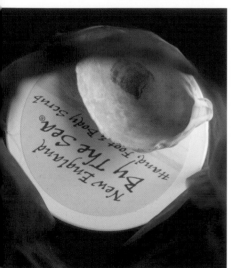

i adore packaging. in the case of *fountain spa & boutique*, the packaging on display gets me every time. all these beautiful lovelies in their boxes and bags, with ribbons and pendants and clever tags. i could never bathe at the pace that i buy shower gels. and if i wore half the makeup i end up buying, i'd look like a lady of the evening. and yet i keep going back, to look and, yes, to buy. *fountain* is just that pretty. and this boutique knows how to lay it out there for greedy eyes like mine.

covet:
sjal eye contour creme
the art of shaving aftershave balm
new england by the sea scrub
mario russo spa soap
tocca wash & delicates bag
erbariva baby cream
massato gel kids hair gel
fantastic spa services

french dressing

dressing for you, your home, and your palate

268 broadway. corner of america
401.272.0441 www.thefrenchdressing.com
tue - sat 11a - 6p sun 11a - 3p

opened in 2004. owner: nadia q. dole
all major credit cards accepted
made-to-order

providence : west side >

french dressing is a very original little boutique with carefully selected items ranging from herbal teas to chunky necklaces to adorable infant clothes. every time i go in, i notice more and more treasures quietly awaiting my attention. i'm told by the owner nadia that she'll be expanding soon and adding a coffee shop. i have no doubt that this, too, will be a place of beauty, with treasures of a different kind.

covet:
lola's toes vintage linen infant smock
salvor graphic printed pigeon t's
sprout salad plant kits
paper treasure leather earrings
woodland spice & tea
wendy baker necklaces

frog & toad

a smorgasbord of fun, smart and attractive gifts and home furnishings

795 hope street. corner of lauriston
401.831.3434
mon - sat 10a - 6p sun noon - 4p

opened in 2001. owners: erin and asher schofield
all major credit cards accepted
personal shopping

providence : hope street > **s12**

i believe there's some backstory to why this shop is called *frog & toad* having to do with the married owners' divergent personalities. or maybe it's just that it's a fondly remembered series featuring sweet stories and illustrations. but really, why am i telling you all this? all you need to know is that if you need a little shopping thrill, a cool watch, say or a killer handbag, or some small touch for your home or a hostess gift, it's all here in the wonderful kaleidoscope of color and texture that is *frog & toad*.

covet:
rhode island soapworks
orange bags by risd students
sukie linens
delilah crown sling bags
cast iron bulldog bottle openers
glazed petal votive holders
frog & toad children's books

galapagos boutique

urbane clothes and shoes

5193 old post road. at route 1
401.322.3000 www.galapagos-boutique.com
mon - sun 8a - 6p

opened in 1996. owners: sandra and david lanning
all major credit cards accepted
alterations/tailoring. personal shopping

charlestown > **s13**

i really am a shoe-crazy mama. for great shoes, i will travel great distances if necessary. in the case of *galapagos boutique*, it is necessary. the store is fairly close to the connecticut border, which means, egads, a 40-minute drive from my pawtucket home. but i'll do it for the olivia rose tals and the other fancy, funky shoes that can be found at this shop. there are other amazing clothes and accessories here, too, and a cozy cofee shop. but for me, it's really all about the shoes.

covet:
alexis bittar necklaces
lipfusion collagen pumping lipliner
passport panties
olivia rose tal silk buckle mules
craig taylor feminine oxford shirts
metal monk semiprecious rings
moo roo ostrich feather handbags

hammen home

a mosaic of clothes, books, novelty and decorative items
62 high street. corner of canal
401.596.3688 www.hammenhome.com
tue - sat 11a - 6p sun noon - 5p

opened in 2002. owners: ellen and bret hammen
all major credit cards accepted

westerly > **s14**

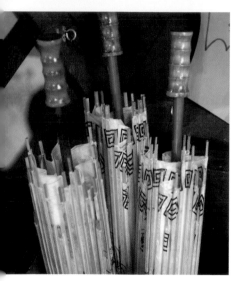

i had my one-year-old daughter vera along with me when i stopped in *hammen home*. i have to give her credit—she only handled one thing while we were in there. i, on the other hand, couldn't stop picking things up. from jewelry to toys to figurine cheese graters to graphic-print t's, there's a little of this and a little of that. and all of it is eminently pickupable.

covet:
tim biskup sketchall bag
poketo deer t's
robotized t's
gary baseman illustrated books
artist series wallets
merricat & me girls' t's
save the queen dresses

house

home decor with beach-y accents
152 mill street. corner of bellevue
401.847.9879
mon - sat 11a - 5:30p sun noon - 5p

opened in 2002. owner: anne foxley
all major credit cards accepted

newport >  **s15**

in my fantasies, i have a beach house. in my fantasy beach house there are real-life items that can be found now at *house*. what well-stocked fantasy beach house doesn't have a giant sand hourglass? or big studded seashell balls? or a cascading capiz chandelier? did i mention that my fantasy beach house comes with a fantasy yacht? i guess i'll have to get busy furnishing that, too. back in reality, it's good to know there's a *house* for your home.

covet:
hable construction gardening gloves
seashell balls
white sand hourglass
elixir vase
paper lace curtains
diptyque feu de bois candle
handpainted newport zip code wall hangings

janet russo

bohemian chic clothing both locally made and collected abroad
154 mill street. corner of bellevue
401.847.9816
mon - fri 11a - 5:30p sat 10a - 6p sun noon - 5p

opened in 2003. owner: janet russo
all major credit cards accepted

newport >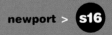

kaie, the creator of these guides, flew out to rhode island to train me in the *eat.shop* style last spring. right after pulling into newport, we stumbled onto *janet russo*. there, i saw kaie whir into action, applauding the cut of a jacket and approving the use of an embroidered detail. for kaie, who's been doing these books at home and abroad, many of the names and collections were familiar and beloved. for me, this was a whole new waiting-to-be-explored world of european flavor and style.

covet:
janet russo everything
kalysta plage tunics
antik batik tunics
miss italy embroidered skirts
nectar jewelry
jamin puech bags
madame a paris tunics

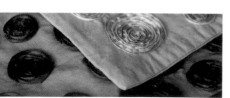

javaspeed

scooter shop and café

1284 n main street. corner of tenth
401.270.9485 www.javaspeed.net
mon 9a - 2p tue 9a - 5p wed - fri 9a - 7p sat 10a - 6p

opened in 2002. owners: patrick engeman and greg woodbury
all major credit cards accepted

providence >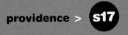

ah, *java speed*. the bad boys who hang here and the women who love them mingle among the vapors of scooter lube, steamed milk, and the "eau de scooter" wafting off the members of the death or glory rally club. if a scooter is not even remotely in your future, you must still come here for the quirkiness and the community and a latte lovingly frothed by owner patty-o. and if you are considering a genuine stella, hurry... they go fast.

covet:
genuine stella scooter
bajaj chetak scooter
kymco scooter from taiwan
tgb scooter from taiwan
brazimoto deerskin green gloves
boom juice coffee boilermaker
message to you root beer

jephry floral studio

creatively arranged flowers and tasteful floral accessories

432 broadway. corner of marshall street
401.351.3510 www.jephry.com
mon - fri 9a - 6p sat 10a - 2p

opened in 1999. owner: jeffrey kerkhoff
all major credit cards accepted

providence : west side > **s18**

sometimes urban living can get to be a drag. that's when i retreat to *jephry floral studio*. granted, it's a flowershop in the middle of westside providence. it offers, however, the finer benefits of the outdoors: fresh, fragrant flowers in full bloom. and there are no pesky bugs to shoo away. then, after your nature hit, you can make someone's day by bringing them an artfully arranged bouquet by the talented jeffrey himself.

covet:
dazzling dahlias
vivid lillies
japanese floral shears
k. hall moss liquid soap
asa porcelain vases
pierced tin lumieres
imported brass frogs

karen vaughn

stylish, fun and one-of-a kind collectibles
148 bellevue avenue. corner of memorial
401.848.2121
mon - sat 10a - 6p sun noon - 6p (call for winter hours)

opened in 1998. owner: karen vaughn
all major credit cards accepted

newport >

the eponymous *karen vaughn* is from the south so she's got the graciousness thing down pat. she also has great taste, likes kids, and has a wicked, slightly blue sense of humor. not coincidentally, in her store you'll find items for a gracious home—one-of-a-kind items from all over the world—a kids' corner, and the occasional off-color double entendre in her labeling. karen vaughn, the person and *karen vaughn*, the store are definitely worth a trip to newport.

covet:
vietnamese wooden cheese graters
cowboy camping-out tent
horsey tuffet
aluminum letters
stingray shagreen bud vase
haitian wooden einstein bowl
red lacquer apothecary cabinet

karol richardson

smashing, super wearable women's clothing
24 washington square. corner of washington
401.849.6612 www.karolrichardson.com
mon - thu 10a - 6p fri - sat 10a - 7p sun 11a - 5p

opened in 1998. owner: karol richardson
all major credit cards accepted
online shopping. alterations/tailoring. personal shopping

newport > **s20**

i brought my friend lisa with me while i was researching *karol richardson*, and in the time that it took to introduce myself to the owners, my fashionista friend had already tried on six or seven amazing pieces. things come that fast and furious when you're at this store. each rack is bursting with gorgeous but wearable clothes that seem suited for the discerning style maven. but one of the nicest things here is that daughter natasha who manages the store radiates with pride when it comes to her hip designer mother, karol. now that's cool.

covet:
karol richardson reversible brocade jacket
rachel weissman wide silk headband
petit pois apple lace skirt cover
kristal larsen textiles wedding dress
streets ahead dyecut leather belt
cynthia rowley equestrian leather bag
rebecca taylor eyelet peasant dress

lazy fish

wonderful collection of something old, something new, something local

235 dodge street. between water street and corn neck road
401.466.2990
mon - tue, thu - fri 10a -3p sat - sun 10a - 5p

opened in 1996. owner: carolyn collins perry
all major credit cards accepted
personal shopping

block island > **s21**

lazy fish lured me in one day at the end of a week-long vacation on block island. maybe I was softened up by several idyllic days of family summer fun. but i walked in and wanted it all. "i'll have one ferry load, please." i managed to get out with a few gifts for others, some etched deco-style souvenir glasses, some neat kid storage boxes, and some cool silkscreened cards. next time, i'm coming in on my first day, not my last.

covet:
vintage pattern shirts
stephen sottile etchings
vintage fish brooches
charlotte herring hand-printed cards
cath kidston "in print" book
pocket paint set
beach scene oils on canvas

lily pad

world furnishings and conversational imports

100 fountain street. corner of matthewson
401.272.1190 www.lilypadhomefurnishings.com
mon - fri 10a - 7p sat 10a - 6p sun noon - 5p

opened in 2006. owner: mark beliveau
all major credit cards accepted
personal shopping

providence : downcity > **s22**

if multi-culti furnishings interest you, as they do me, but you feel crowded in some of the major import stores, as i do, then *lily pad* will hit the spot. i'm interested in seeing what comes off of these container ships, but i can't stomach the vast visual clutter that is the norm in the big stores. by contrast, mark carefully edits the items in his store, and the result is a select number of ever-changing, always interesting pieces.

covet:
sara weiss mother-of-pearl bracelets
tibetan singing bowls
feng shui chart
ostrich eggs from new zealand
peruvian gourd birdhouses
spotted leopard tea
plantation reclining chair

little bits

children's clothing with style and a mission

134 spring street. corner of church
401.848.0059 www.littlebits.com
winter: mon - sat 10a - 5p sun noon - 5p
summer: mon - sat 10a - 6p sun 11a - 6p

opened in 2004. owner: monica rodgers
all major credit cards accepted
online shopping. made to order. personal shopping

newport > **s23**

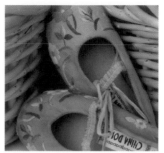

when i had my daughter gwen, we had the ugliest car seat. everybody did. but at least ours was subdued. it was just grey checked. imagine a pink and perfect poppet stashed in a boring gray seat. it was like putting the hope diamond in a rusted tin setting. i complained about it. *little bits* owner monica felt the same way, but she actually did something about it, creating a series of playful and washable car seat covers. this charming store is an offshoot of that first venture. smart.

covet:
little bits moma-dot car seat cover
tiny bubbles monogrammed pants with ric-rac
belt with wonderboy buckle
the clique shift
tea world collection infant clothes
be maternity & infant line
holtztiger wooden collectible figures

madre bella

stylish maternity, nursing and infant clothes
one waseca avenue. at route 114
401.247.0122
mon - sat 10a -5p sun by appointment

opened in 2005. owner: rebecca freitas
all major credit cards accepted

barrington >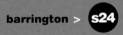

by the time this book hits shelves, *madre bella* store owner rebecca will have delivered her first child. let's hope that this dose of reality doesn't affect her sense of style. *madre bella* is stocked with gorgeous, flattering clothes for well-dressed and sexy moms-to-be. i trust these outfits will not give way to the easy wash, perma-press, barf-concealing, neutral-patterned clothes that new moms fall prey to. let expectant mothers keep their fantasies and dress to the nines—viva la sexy mama.

covet:
samson martin sassy t's
chiara kruza sequin disco dress
momzee maternity halter top
tiny bubbles brown & turquoise dresses
luvbug design soft blankets
kiwi industries hooded sweatshirts

martina & company

european and local contemporary jewelry

120 n main street. corner of thomas
401.351.0968 www.martina-company.com
tue - wed, fri 11a - 6p thu 11a - 7p sat 10a - 5p

opened in 1998. owner: martina windels
all major credit cards accepted
made to order

providence > **s25**

so, i go into *martina & company* and i start taking pictures of all the beautiful pieces, asking about all of the designers, learning a bit about current trends from owner martina's native germany, hearing about the jewelry courses at risd, and finding out many other noteworthy facts. but what i don't know until i'm practically walking out the door, courtesy of martina's european humility, is that martina herself is a serious and much-honored designer. my advice to you is to examine all the lovely items up front but make sure to ask to see martina's things, too.

covet:
martina windels jack earrings
heather guidero necklace
steelyard nail earrings
karen gilbert glass necklace
annika harms coral & pearl necklace
lena hulsmeier lenticular bracelets & earrings
dahlia kanner earrings

mignonette

eclectic and luxe women's boutique

301 wickenden street. corner of brook street
401.272.4422 www.mignonette.net
mon - sat 11a - 6p sun noon - 5p

opened in 2002. owner: tara solon
all major credit cards accepted
personal shopping.

providence : wickenden st. >

talking to *mignonette* owner tara reminds me of that '80s song by m that began: "london, paris, new york, munich, everybody talk about pop music." all her romantic, exquisite, unusual and hard-to-find items spring from all corners of the world, and the references to her travel punctuates each story. the store itself has charming clusters representing an array of world cities. and the vibe: the last time i visited, liza was fluttering her giant eyelashes in cabaret on a big plasma screen while a bollywood song supplied the sound. perfection.

covet:
mor bath line soak
truefitt & hill shaving line for men
bond no. 9 perfumes
emma hope tapestry shoes
cath kidston clothespin holders
london & paris dance cd imports
elle mcpherson lingerie

ocean state tackle

bait living, dead, and inanimate in a stylish tackle shop setting

430 branch avenue. corner of charles
401.751.4827 www.oceanstatetackle.com
mon - sat 5a - 8p sun 5a - 6p

opened in 2002. owner: david henault
all major credit cards accepted
online shopping

providence > **s27**

this place is great a bait-and-tackle shop with high-design sensibilities. when *ocean state tackle* first opened, with its trademark fish painted along the facade, i thought it was some snarky new seafood restaurant. oh, there are fish inside, to be sure: squirming, wriggling pogies, minnows, and eels who will end up dunked in the bay to catch some larger, tastier fish. you'll also find a rainbow of lures, fishing line, bobbers, and etcetera related to the pastime. if fishing's your thing, talk to dave. he'll hook you up.

covet:
okuma fin-chaser rod
st. croix reel
temple fork outfitters rod case
readyfish aluminum gaff
ocean state tackle cotton weathered hat
clam worms
live pogies

pelle nuda

products for a pampered lifestyle
224 water street. between chapel and high
401.466.5252
mon - fri 10a - 9p sat - sun 9a - 9p

opened in 2006. owner: kara sasso
mc. visa

block island > **s28**

pelle nuda hadn't opened when we last vacationed on block island, and that's probably a good thing... for my budget. showcased within an otherwise plain building is a beautiful and sophisticated array of bath, beauty and candle products. i was most tickled by a lumière candle with the scent of clothesline. send out your laundry, but keep the clothesline burning.

covet:
korres makeup
bliss body buff
the art of bathing calm evening salts
lumière clothesline candle
rivale grapefruit fig soap
jimmy cremesicle soy candles
davies gate sweet orange firming masque

relish

great variety of housewares and decorative items

377 broadway. corner of andrew
401.273.8883 www.relishprovidence.com
tue - sat 11a - 6:30p sun 11a - 4p

opened in 2004. owners: laura hirsch and stephen pancerev
mc. visa

providence : west side > **s29**

my first time in *relish*, i felt a certain sense of comfort. even to the untrained eye, this is clearly a haven for fun and funky housewares, clothing, and jewelry. but what would account for the quiet happy feeling i was having? a discussion with owner laura solved the mystery. laura, like me, is from portland, oregon. her sensibilities and even some of her art hail from there. but mixed in are fine gifts from all over, including plenty from rhode island artists. to my mind, *relish* combines the best offerings of west and east and a bunch in between.

covet:
perch bird lamps
miele fresca t's
pamela barsky journals
amie plante lily of the valley earrings
k-studio pillows
korres body care
heather guidero costume jewelry

rocket to mars

floor-to-ceiling vintage goodness
144 broadway. corner of dean
401.274.0905
wed - fri 11a - 6p sat noon - 6p sun noon - 5p

opened in 2003. owners: jennifer ricci and dennis cooper
mc. visa
will purchase single items or whole estates

providence : west side > **s30**

rocket to mars is just good, clean, archetypal vintage: atomic-era relics and childhood memories in plastic, lucite and needlepoint. seems to me the approach to vintage has changed in the last few years. yesterday's need to do your whole house in the truman or kennedy era has been replaced by the more measured approach of blending select bits from the '50s, '60s, '70s and '80s. when you need that just-so lamp, ashtray or chair, rocket over to broadway.

covet:
vintage barkcloth linens
plastic spaghetti pendants
phone table
rocket table lamps
big ash trays
draft horse vases

roy

astoundingly beautiful tableware and gifts

221 spring street. corner of prospect hill
401.849.9258 www.fredroy.com
thu - sun noon - 5p

opened in 2004. owners: fred & nancy olsen roy
all major credit cards accepted
made to order. personal shopping

newport > **s31**

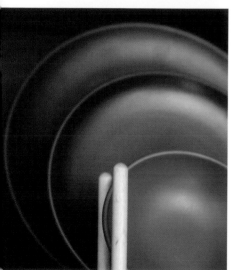

roy is the antidote to the "too much stuff" syndrome often found in the bigger homegoods stores. the store is small and neat and everything within radiates clean lines, and a consistent eye. while there i felt like i was in a temple of good design. for consumerists like myself, this is practically religion. it might be time to tithe some of my income to the roy coffers.

covet:
dermond peterson wood block
  printed cocktail napkins
match italian pewter & porcelain dinnerware
match hand cast butter bell
edith heath tea set
faux flokati throws
riedel bar glasses

seaport studios

preppy and resort wear for kids and their grownups

122 bay street. at fort road
401.348.9010 www.seaport-studios.com
may 1 - oct 15 mon - sun 10a - 9p

opened in 1984. owners: jean saunders and perry kellogg
all major credit cards accepted

westerly > s32

like a moth to flame, i cannot resist admiring little kids' shoes. in fact, i was nearly done in by the offerings on display at *seaport studios*. first, i couldn't get enough of the infant reef flip-flops. i repeat: infant flip-flops! then i poked around and uncovered all kinds of cute clothes and beach-inspired gifts for kids. i know that *seaport* has a similar store in the back, stocked with just as many irresistibles for grownups... but who can walk away from the teeny tiny flip-flops?

---

covet:
greggy girl two-piece jumper set
woody model cars
reef infant flip-flops
straw studio bags
spotty headbands
personalized vintage-style beach plaques

7 ply

surfing and skating lifestyle offerings

3 canal street. corner of high
401.348.0656 www.7ply.com
mon - fri 11a - 7p sat 10a - 6p sun 11a - 6p

opened in 1998. owners: ted and heather rice
mc. visa

westerly >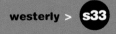

7 ply has that air of coolness that compels you to pull over and check it out. at least that's what i did when i saw its big big signage. it is a mega-surf and skate lifestyle shop housed in a former cvs. and while i neither surf nor skate, the inventory here is compelling enough from a design standpoint to make me want to check it out. if it's seductive to me, imagine how great it is for south county's many committed surfers and skaters.

covet:
obey t's
hurley low ride bermudas
etnies low-slip v
xcel wetsuits
exile skimboard
upper playground wear
oakley fives 3.0 sunglasses

shoreline

variety of youthful, outdoorsy clothes and accessories
238 ocean avenue. near beach avenue
401.466.5800
mon - fri 10a - 8p sat - sun 9a - 8p (summer season and christmas)

opened in 1982. owner: danielle duffy
all major credit cards

block island > **s34**

i have never been confused with a sporty person. really. therefore, i present *shoreline* as a service to those of you who may be sporty but not without style. many of the clothes here are functional and designed for outdoor wear, but a number of them are hella fun, too. take the swim trunks with over-sized pockets for holding drinks. or the cute raffia sun visor. could this be the beginning of jan, the sporty type?

covet:
the matix supergusto party pants
dvs flip flops
goorin field & stream baseball cap
french coil rings
blue no. 7 ice bags
the yoga cap shower cap
molle cram cream school totebag

simple pleasures

beautiful, refined and quirky objects

6 richmond square. corner of waterman
401.331.4120 www.simplepleasuresprovidence.com
tue - sat 11a - 6p

opened in 1992. owner: mary moore
all major credit cards

providence : wayland square > **s35**

situated in a tiny 19th century forge building beside the seekonk river, *simple pleasures* is, quite simply, one of the loveliest shops you'll ever see from the outside. yet on the inside, it manages somehow to be even lovelier. graciously stocked with beautiful things, the tables are laid out in that seemingly casual way that speaks volumes about mary's talent for design and display. this is also a store that, for me, is impossible to leave empty-handed. the pleasures may be simple, but they abound here.

covet:
barbara schriber pennants
moon tide tie-dyed cotton shirts
tea forte silken infusers
saipua mango butter body soap
rhinestone crowns
alexander moore outdoor furniture
eva solo bird feeders

spoiled little ones

double-threat boutique for kids and pets

36 main street. between division and melrose
401.398.7711 www.spoiledlittleones.com
tue - sat 10a - 6p or by appointment

opened in 2006. owner: stacy ramey
mc. visa
personal shopping

east greenwich > **s36**

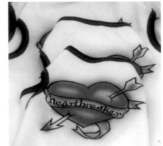

i have a weird aversion to dog bakeries. it's not that i have any inherent problem with them, it's just that they frequently seem to fail, and that makes me sad. i might worry, too, about a high-end dog boutique, except for the master stroke that sets this one apart. *spoiled little ones* is not just for spoiled pets, but spoiled little humans too. quel combination! onesies for dogs and babies. leashes and bibs. no-tear and no-matte shampoos. who doesn't have a pet and a nephew? genius!

covet:
walk e woo collars & leashes
i see spot magnet dog t's
happytails fur butter
kee ka wearable greetings
"confucius say" dog bowl
egg baby dress
dogo chic carrying bags

store four

european-style cookware and tableware offerings

673 kingstown road. corner of old tower hill
401.783.7388 www.storefour.net
wed - sat 10a - 5p or by appointment

opened in 2005. owner: ellen cesario
all major credit cards accepted
made-to-order. personal shopping

wakefield > **s37**

store four at first sight just looks like a lot of fun. already stocked with a wide variety of nifty tabletop stuff, it is scheduled to start offering classes and demonstrations in its open kitchen soon. perhaps because it is run by a mother and daughter team, the conversations around the big bench table are sure to be comfortable and chatty. i can imagine just hanging out here on a stool, learning and gabbing, and—knowing me—buying.

covet:

les confitures a l'ancienne jams

mario batali persimmon enamel dutch oven

catstudio rhode island embroidered pillow

jill fenichell plastic plates

moroccan-made tagines

boston ceramic salt pig

voluspa cardamom fig candle

strada

stylish shoes with an emphasis on comfort
185 wayland avenue. corner of medway
401.272.1935 www.strada-shoes.com
mon - wed 10a - 6p thu - fri 10a - 8p sat 10a - 6p sun noon - 5p

opened in 2002. owners: william and anna clark
all major credit cards accepted

providence : wayland square > **s38**

there will always be occasions for crazily elevated stilettos. but have you ever tried chasing kids around in those? especially in the back yard. in the best case you end up aerating your lawn, and worst-case, twisting an ankle. so it's good that *strada* has found its niche, selling high-quality, comfort shoes that don't settle on style. and never fear, *strada* has a fantastic selection of sexy, aerating heels also.

covet:
terra peck graphic black & white wedge
rieker anti-stress tennis shoes
pikolinos of spain embroidered slingbacks
luisa d'orio pastel sandals
peter kaiser faux croc pumps
rieker buckle mary janes
kent stetson handmade purses

studio hop

fine art, furnishings, jewelry and antiques
810 hope street. corner of fourth
401.621.2262
mon - sat 10a - 6p sun 11a - 3p (closed sundays july and august)

opened in 2000. owners: nina and peter tegu
all major credit cards accepted
made to order. personal shopping

providence : hope street >

i should probably just keep a tab at *studio hop*. here's the equation: it's near my home + it stocks great mid-priced, one-of-a-kind art and jewelry = this is where i buy all my birthday gifts for friends and relatives. i imagine that the first of my friends to receive a handmade leather wrist cuff with bakelite buckle felt flattered. by the fifth time i gave one out, i think word had spread. hey, no matter how many friends i buy it for, this is still a great gift and a great gift store.

covet:
ellen mayer leather cuffs with bakelite buckles
kat dalene silver draped chain necklace
aster & sage pillows
sam ames watermelon oil on canvas
rag & bone handmade journals
mio studio exotic wood & sterling necklace
taleen batalian oil & encaustic painting

the glass station

watch your own glass item being created
318 main street. corner of robinson
401.788.2500 www.ebenhortonglass.com
mon - sat 10a - 6p sun 10a - 3p (closed mon jan - may 1)

opened in 1999. owners: eben horton and woodi woodring
all major credit cards accepted
made to order

wakefield >

rhode island is home to many glass artists, but with three kids under six, i don't—surprise—spend a lot of time in the galleries. what's cool about *the glass station*, though, is that they make their pieces inside a former gas station, with the big garage doors thrown open. this way, big and small can watch from a safe distance as the artisans twirl and hammer the molten glass into clever and eye-catching pieces. this is performance art for all ages.

covet:
wave vases
squid art piece
ribbon paperweight
pinecone paperweight
gourd-style bud vase
iridescent ornaments
wavy bowls

trappings

wonderfully subversive preppy gear
474 thames street. corner of extension
401.849.9898
mon - sun 10a - 9p

opened in 2006. owner: jennifer casner
all major credit cards accepted
made to order

newport >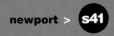

"no preppy!" i barked at my friend when she joined me for some scouting in newport. "i will not feature a preppy store," i maintained. "you can't make me," i insisted. then i walked into *trappings*. brilliant, hilarious *trappings*. it takes your basic boilerplate preppy and gives it the funnest, freshest, most subversive spin. the clothes are fabulous, the shoes are pure delight. we closed down the place that evening, and i was still finding pink and green treats on every shelf.

covet:
fifi tee's anchor t-shirt
hadley potter canvas belt bags
rapunzel dress espadrilles
anna william quilted bags
jojo oversized bauble bracelet & earrings
skirtin around silk print dress
b. tara design terry short wrap

wendy brown linens

bed, bath & beautiful things
183 wayland avenue. between angell and waterman
401.455.2337 www.wendybrownlinens.com
mon - sat 10a - 5p

opened in 2000. owner: wendy brown
all major credit cards accepted
made to order. personal shopping

providence : wayland square > **s42**

i now own a lampe berger. before i went into *wendy brown linens*, i hadn't even heard of lampe berger. but wendy assured me they're all the rage and told me a little about the history of these bacteria-eating, scent-wafting, decorative porcelain pieces. this is what i love about this shop—wendy is on top of all this stuff. now i don't have to go to italy to get the finest linens or to japan for the best toothpaste. i only have to come to wayland square.

covet:
modern style lampe berger
wiggy studio dupione baby hat
sferra bros. italian linens
breath palette japanese toothpaste
michael weems napkins
stephanie johnson raffia bag
le blanc linen wash

etc.

the eat.shop guides were created by kaie wellman and are published by cabazon books
for more information about the series: www.eatshopguides.com

eat.shop.rhode island was written, researched and photographed by jan faust
the guide was edited by kaie wellman

copy editing: lynn king   fact checking: pat de garmo
map design and production: ligature laboratories - kieran lynn, jim anderson, erin cheek and kate emmons

jan thx: all the businesses featured in this book. to kaie for her vision and great management. to my mom for, well, everything. to anna, gail and lisa, great friends all and each stylishly unique. to my dear children gwen, johnny and vera.

this book is dedicated to abe, with love.

cabazon books: eat.shop.rhode island
ISBN 0-9766534-4-3

every effort has been made to ensure the accuracy of the information in this book. however, certain details are subject to change. please remember when using the guides that hours alter seasonally and some-times sadly, businesses close. the publisher cannot accept responsibility for any consequences arising from the use of this book.

the eat.shop guides are distributed by independent publishers group: www.ipgbook.com

PRINTED IN SINGAPORE